THE BODY COUNTRY

THE BODY COUNTRY
SUSIE ANDERSON

Megan, how nice to meet
you in person finally!
I hope you like the
poems x Susie

hachette
AUSTRALIA

This manuscript won State Library of Queensland's black&write! Fellowship.

Published in Australia and New Zealand in 2023
by Hachette Australia
(an imprint of Hachette Australia Pty Limited)
Gadigal Country, Level 17, 207 Kent Street, Sydney, NSW 2000
www.hachette.com.au

Hachette Australia acknowledges and pays our respects to the past, present and
future Traditional Owners and Custodians of Country throughout Australia
and recognises the continuation of cultural, spiritual and educational practices
of Aboriginal and Torres Strait Islander peoples. Our head office is located on
the lands of the Gadigal people of the Eora Nation.

 A catalogue record for this
book is available from the
National Library of Australia

ISBN: 978 0 7336 4982 0 (paperback)

Cover design by Alex Ross
Cover photographs courtesy of Kseniya Gunina-Averburg and Victoria Burt / Alamy and
h.yegho / Shutterstock
Author photograph courtesy of the author
Typeset in 12/16.5 pt Bembo Pro by Bookhouse, Sydney
Printed and bound in Australia by McPherson's Printing Group

MIX
Paper | Supporting
responsible forestry
FSC® C001695

The paper this book is printed on is certified against the
Forest Stewardship Council® Standards. McPherson's Printing
Group holds FSC® chain of custody certification SA-COC-005379.
FSC® promotes environmentally responsible, socially beneficial
and economically viable management of the world's forests.

To my teachers.

Contents

time, place, country

embrace	5
sunday feeling	6
leave early	7
silent / song	9
tiddas	11

chorus

bulabul	*ants*	19
gurug	*magpie*	20
djubi-djubi	*small bird*	21
djinab	*cockatoo*	22
gauir	*emu*	23
mindjun	*grey kangaroo*	25
gurn-gurn	*kookaburra*	26
werbil	*eagle*	27

when artists talk about country

dress code	31
sidney nolan	33
counter narrative	34
unceremonious	35
connecting	36
favourite artwork	38

go within

surveillance   48

silent way   49

perfect alphabet   51

9.14 (68) – 10.8 (68)   52

solipsism, or a little death   53

jupiter & venus   54

the fatalist   55

zodiac buzz-killer   57

the water not the wave

blacktown   63

warrane   64

merri   65

lake people i   66

lake people ii   67

lake people iii   68

lake people iv   69

territories

authority figures   75

revolve   78

to yoke   79

how to fall in love with your home town   80

territory   81

afterword   85

Wergaia Language words   89

acknowledgements   91

time, place, country

boundaries of Country are rivers
mountains
sea

boundaries of body are longevity
endurance
tenacity

boundaries of love are care
capacity
energy

but
love
also
knows
no
boundary

3

embrace

when I return the air bites
asking *where you been*
bush nags my clothing and
each prickle torn from shoelace
stings punishment for absence
mist rolls across mountain
named by homesick Scottish
it's been Gariwerd longer
morning sunbeams whisper
willy wagtail gossip
every rustle makes me jump
I thought no one was around
but there always was someone here
timeless mountain range
shoulders this land I love
sitting still and solitary
inhale   exhale
nothing else is quite so fixed
heavy with thousands of years
become part of atmosphere

sunday feeling

evening sunset by the lake sent
shadows through half-clothed trees
maybe fire burning bright beyond town
but mum said it was just paddocks gleaming
shepherd's delight. faded signs
in twilight, broken play equipment
and rickety fences reminded us
everything was wrong in the world.

winter had been dry and town was crunchy
the paper said children under five
wouldn't know what rain was. no river
water flowed and trees shed crispy
bark broke well underfoot.

mum brought presents from the city, but
instead of newness, everything could have
gone down with the sun. burn up
in flames. no one else around
as we crunched leaves, an empty sunday
walk through rundown tennis courts
and abandoned CFA training areas.

leave early

we always sat with the boys
up back of the bus. our world neat
paddock grids, edges ever visible.

fire season years later blew through
boundaries. wind changed direction
and the plan was leave early.

no neighbours lost lives or houses
but land incinerated hundreds.
sheep burnt before their time.

farmers dug pits of blackened soil
excavating earth for charred carcasses
unaware what they had already extracted.

similarities so small now, distant
and past. our differences spread out
across years taking up space

boys from the bus now horrified
grown men digging mass graves
gathering remains with tractors.

the body was just a temporary, lonely container that I happened
to be borrowing

the book meant the body was container for the self
I feel like self is slippery and wants to be untethered
from the world
will do anything it can to get liminal

the self wants to know what the light was doing

how shadows fell

how clouds opened

how sun felt on skin

silent / song
for Lutruwita, during Dark Mofo 2017

i

I was right about that place. It was winter
colourless to the core, apart from sunset
that bled siren song across horizon.

The same ache draws our gaze upwards again
and again. Called skywards we have no explanation
for her, so what is the sound? Some heard a cry
for help but to me that was a refrain of hope.

ii

At Kunanyi granite spoke as we fell silent.
What is it that hushed us, the landscape
haunted by a history of forgetting? Or our own
mortality echoing loudly across the scree.

iii

I am silent just like the golden of home,
rustling long and wide up Country.

Once I thought I could speak the land,
more consonants than vowel,
yet the letters don't feel right
and I can't hear the sound.

tiddas

gums in headlights
mum drives home
after many wines
and one coffee
empty country roads
swerving for fun
cassette up loud
searching for mopoke
every silver tree
cold backseat wearing
her big jumper
maybe we will
never get home

what to do . . .

be part of something bigger
hear the ancestral lines speak
more connected yet clearly less one 'self'

listen for shadows

see warmth

hear clouds

the body is just a container
containing me
a channel or conduit for story

chorus

new tattoo in the middle of my back
wing with red swipe through the centre
inscriptions
mark how incredible the body presence is
red and black ink settling
a commemoration
movement from within becomes memorial on the outside

forget subtle challenges of the body
remember to feel
ancestral connection beyond
here and now

Mum says they move faster when rain comes. For me they're wound up with that beautiful word petrichor.

But of course ants have their very own smell.

If the earth looks loose, shifting, almost in motion, you can be sure it's their battleground. They're always there, but seem to be more noticeable in the summer. That's when they break in to find treasures in the house. Nuisance for us. Goldmine for them.

They will carry almost anything.

The other day I noticed one marching past carrying half a bee. Its body. Stamen?

gurug   *magpie*

It's not quiet here. Constant echo of calls between trees. Bouncing around different heights and positions.

What on earth could they be going on about? Perhaps that rain is on the way.

As you can see, ink is starting to run on the page.

djubi-djubi   *small bird*

There are many prize feathers to collect. I have just
added a blue wren's to my collection. The others:
robin red-breast, cockatoo, galah, kookaburra.

Often the males sport splendid coloured suits.
Females dress down.

One flew inside the other day and couldn't get out.
This isn't your house, we said, let us show you the
way. We coaxed the brown bird from the sewing
room.

I thought I might have to clasp her in my hands.
But the frightened wren nearly flew into the mirror,
coming face to face with the end. Lucky she realised
just in time.

We opened the kitchen window, removed the fly
wire and she escaped.

I had so wanted to hold that little bird.

djinab   *cockatoo*

Screeching tears the sky apart. A massive rip
ricocheting through blue, clouds hiding a seam
(instinct to write 'to the heavens' but actually) to
beyond. Clouds hiding a seam.

These white feathers are strong. Viscous. A prize to
find one unattached to a bird. For a headdress, or a
crown.

To crown.

I heard there are cockatoos who live a very long
time. Up to fifty years in captivity. How much
more, or less, I wonder, in the wild. That's just the
white ones. Black ones are rarer here. But I've made
sure they're with me always, inked in my skin.

Triangle footprints through the paddock, toes in the dirt road, feathers in the barbed wire fence. In the southeast we track emu to sky and back again.

One mythological memory of long ago. Drives with dad out on different jobs. On the neighbour's property near the reservoir, base of the fire tower. Emerging into a clearing we found emu eggs. Did he know to find nests there (who would I ask)? Massive yolks slid from navy blue shell.

More, other different egg times after he'd died.

Before the adults could blow the yolks to make trophies, we snatched them to smash underneath the trampoline. The trampoline was simultaneously a prop, the stage, the star. All our performances took place there.

But first, the smashing.

We would upend it so the long edge was on the grass. Get a good run up, jump and cling on, falling backwards as it righted itself again. The elastic part always looked terrifying on the run up but relented in the come down, springy and forgiving. The bars, however, could be vicious, which we knew from our egg exploits. Hands and feet had to be well clear of them, just like from the coils themselves. Give you a nasty pinch if you weren't careful.

Through this routine many eggs met their end. Or it may have just been once and relived many times.

Other performances were staged on the trampoline. Its shiny black surface allowed slipping and sliding, while rounded corners were perfect wings, just like in real theatre. All these aspects were used in our major hit 'The Emu Crossed the Road'.

I'd be a lesser woman if I pretended I didn't remember how it went.

It was a highly physical number.

mindjun   *grey kangaroo*

They move slowly and carefully. Lolloping along.
Then they move very very fast. Could have been a
person hiding in the trees. A quick getaway.

On this land I always imagine it's a person with a
secret. Hiding some family knowledge. Hiding my
father, as if death hadn't disappeared him off this
earth.

An old grey fella visits us most nights. Comes very
close to the house. Watching, moving slowly, and
bolting if we come outside.

I walk through paddocks looking for any sign of
life. Tail swipes mark the dirt. Grey shadows that
look like landscape shifting—part of the paddock—
become forms darting off into the scrub.

If it's him, I wonder, why would he run?

gurn–gurn   *kookaburra*

Every now and then, offstage, a whirring starts. It
begins like a surprise, but the confidence that erupts
next erases any doubt they've come in before or
after their cue.

It could be laughter as they say, but it's a cry of a
different order. Rumbling from somewhere else
completely.

That mountain sits and observes like the bird chorus
around us. What it could sing. Could it help me get
my voice back?

There was a time when sound tumbled out of my
throat like kookaburra's. Natural. Hurried but
unforced. Trills creating unique phrases.

I mean singing. But I don't just mean singing. I've
clammed up in more ways than one.

werbil   *eagle*

Very high up at cloud's edge. A couple.

I'm always searching for their two dots. They fly all
the way up and down the range. Mum says I've got
good eyesight. I can spot them.

Sure, I can find them, but I miss other things.

I do not know what I miss.
Was familiar.
It was.

Two eagles.
Not to be confused with whistling kites.
Eagles go higher.

Til they're just a speck gradually moving across sky.

when artists talk about country

dress code
after Amala Groom

Sis, who are you
I am not ready to be tied down

Sis, what are you running from
I'm not running I'm pulling myself toward distance

Sis, where are you trying to go
I'm not trying

Sis, why are you holding on
I'm not holding on I have a firm grip of myself

Sis, how are you going to get there
In a dress

       Sis, who are you
       I am unknown

     Sis, what are you running from
     I am running towards the knowable

      Sis, where are you trying to go
      I am going to where I am known

Sis, why are you holding on
I am holding on to what I know

Sis, how are you going to get there
In my dress

                          Sis, who are you
                          I won't be defined

                    Sis, what are you running from
                               I won't tell

                    Sis, where are you trying to go
                    This isn't what going looks like

                          Sis, why are you holding on
                          This is just a guideline

              Sis, how are you going to get there
                               In this dress

sidney nolan

here is not familiar Country
I love what I see but don't recognise
anyone who has spent time with this land knows
the gleaming is practical
fields either side of well-worn roads
driven after school or between runs
to ballet class or piano lessons
site of harvest
so memory empties when called forth
mostly silent or low to ground among
peaks of earlier times blurred now with loss
where has this peach, this red come from?
plains echo ancestral
he must have meant an everyday blend
gold and grey with blue haze horizon
gestural motion of strokes rings true at least
recalls heat of endless January
giving every direction its own pulse
I long to inhabit that edge

counter narrative

see here how each silvery gum
glows as if a spectre, lumped
with more shadowy figures
seeming on the verge
interrupting otherwise rolling
hills with spindly gothic extremities, leering
canvas merging with paddock
swirls of sky and birds at once intensely
becoming same—move quickly
to next room but more of the same
grief embedded into landscape
more tall trees obscuring the farmer
his failures make no sense here
no ruins to make this allegorical or
mythological fear instead it's a bicentennial
of untamed darkness incessant, immutable
roaring nature, waiting to be divided

unceremonious

after Nicole Foreshew

at first glance this was just seven or eight
different types of branches, or sticks, arranged
shortest to tallest but moving further into the room
a glint, a glimmer drew you closer to reveal treasure
hugging knots of the branches, grown into
the black and grey crevices and grown on top of
each other, cabinet ready, specimen-like,
a living fossil or echoing wood petrified—
branches formerly known as trees petrified—
minerals cultivated by the artist
over several visits to Country
she called the mixture her secret potion
ground plus time becomes a natural incubator
now, to reconsider what we extract from
earth, how land is used, what can be grown
or taken from place, exploring edges of materiality

connecting

(to create frequencies)

earth moves wavering uncertainty colour
undulates and shifts in opposition to all
we hold to be true the truest fact the stable
ground will outlast us touch these parts
ancient land feel the others knowing
who was here before visitors think it untouched
patterns nobody else has known the quiet
a kind nobody else has heard what could
this sound look like I am so much less
than a mountain but still we are of it

(love that rests as potentiality emerges)

once fully open these eyes seek across
and beyond to see into another pair
insurmountable not sure why people reach
for me perhaps I've been reaching first
arms outstretched in case this time coalescence
which must be let in even knowing it will fade
away like everything does so beautifully
how else to make sense of this and the world
in a beautiful way just hanging on for
final moment of dissolve into pure beauty

proximity to Country creates bodily equilibrium
and a sense of deep peace within

physical presence on Country
becomes care for the self
becomes interior romantic love

favourite artwork
for Redrock

storm paints barks lilac watercolour
rainfall brushing mountain deeper red
false starts of spring renewal

it's a shame their name ignores
the silver sheen, but now I've lost
I know exactly why they're blue gums

pelicans curl elastic necks backward
while their smaller cousins flap pointlessly
suspended by wind

swaying reeds grasp for a hand
sun dissolves into horizon
day's rhythm over and over again

my mistake was looking for stars
and seeing only brightness
not what was between

night sky maps Country onto lake
reflection holds knowledge
celestial canvas of kinship and story

the body will be written by time
it will not always keep you
we become land immemorial

merging with Country forever
born from dust
return to ochre dust

get more abstract tattoos
ink this down
it sounds like a joke and it is but it's also not

even the abstracted means something
staking a literal claim on this actual body of mine

container marked red for ochre
marked black for blak
becoming my most sovereign self

at least that one thing is for sure

go within

let me try this

you know how the mania of a romance works?

that is the otherworldly connection and attraction to our
homelands
inexplicable in the same way

desire to care
less speakable than words
stronger than articulation

love is not just contained in a singular human body
it becomes a place
created between

two bodies
(sometimes one person is tending the place more)

imagine
the interior Country

we desire always to be connected to our ancestral lands
and have sovereignty over them .

cultural body
knowledge-body
sovereign body and self

the ultimate desire

surveillance

When you take a photo with your phone
it tracks your location precisely.
There was one photo of us actually
looking like a couple. We were
walking through Fitzroy North and you
were going to that girl's house but
I was being cool and pretending
I didn't mind at all. Exact details
saved with the file: mid–May,
just before midnight, even the street name.
There was a cat nearby and I patted it.
You took photos of me, hair falling
onto the cat's body, as I lovingly held it.
Strange, you then made us take pictures
together. Our faces are tinged
street-lamp yellow. Our eyes filled
with the following: you upset me,
I forgive you, I lose myself.

silent way

i

all talk is translation. I mean, listening is translation.
there are twenty-six different symbols for
misunderstanding what you meant. there's the order
they're put down in vs the order they arranged into once
they reached my eyes. screened. filtered.

ii

avoiding music with lyrics so all these thoughts can take
up space.

iii

the broken record is words you spoke with your mouth.
on repeat with your laugh and what your hands were
capable of. feel it making you come alive. in the quietest
place, in a silent way, making a void. with no space
between them you know what those last two words
become.

iv

space: problem and solution at once. also the name of my
ambient music playlist.

v

you found it. the poem that's about you.

vi

no longer longing, absence of sound brings comfort,
but there's always and still the breath. that's still sound.
coming to a sound still. that void was mine to face all
along and all alone. how the heart reads the gaps over
and over again.

perfect alphabet

I heard the shape of Korean language characters is the
way the mouth looks when forming the sounds. Can
you think of a more sensible way to make a language?
Your pillow lips narrow into a straight line. There is no
sound. Only a coin flipping over and over in my nervous
hands. Each turn gives us another chance. You say 'once
something is said it is lost forever' and it's true, the words
dissolve before me. If I could have seen your lips once
more I would have written down their shape.

9.14 (68) – 10.8 (68)

One of those years the AFL grand final was a draw. It was so surreal to all the fans it may have happened in a parallel universe. They left the stadium sombre, unmoored. The city clouded over in response to the subdued crowds even though it was early in spring. It was the same night you came to my small apartment. Still I believe if I'd kissed you then I could have changed everything. It feels now like it happened to another person: droves of confused faces and your voice whispering stories in my ear. Some days I look at the sky honestly seeing it as the same one you are under. Beyond that blue there is nothing. I protect myself from understanding that fully by loving cloud, sun and star. It's all right there. Why anyone would go into space is literally beyond me.

solipsism, or a little death

Chaos is king, and this morning
everything fell apart everywhere
in the train carriage.
Out from any available orifice
came memory, emotion, feeling
along with piss and shit and blood.
this relief spread through the
carriage and I became serene.
People simply continued their morning
commute. I wanted to wrest phones
from hands, throw them on the ground.
Women would avert their eyes rather
than help, rather sneak a picture of
my entrails as they alight the train.
Yet I still walk about, detached
from everything in a most pleasant way.
both my aunts said *if you don't laugh
you'll cry.* Somehow it is all there again
every day. Here is a hand, mouth that opens,
somehow sounds that make words still
tumble out. I keep looking at the stars
to see the universe, but the joke is
I am the universe.

jupiter & venus

It was big news: they would be closer to each other
than ever before. At night walking
in the middle of the road I could see the two planets
like I was told. It seemed they had arrived together,
but were already disappearing at different speeds.
With a telescope maybe you could see Jupiter's moons.
Mum called to talk about her life,
we remarked about the planets. All echoes
on the street look at the sky, empty
apart from two bright beacons. The arc
their proximity, thirteen months of courting.
When would I forget to notice their devotion,
how we are closeness. Venus has been falling
lower into the sky every night since.

the fatalist

last night on the plane I felt doomed
in a calm way. we boarded via a bus
and some eastern europeans sang as
we climbed the stairs and I thought
I'm going to die with these people
singing foreign songs around me.
I wanted to judge them but changed
my mind—at least they were laughing
and happy—global human behaviour
warms the heart, their holiday in-joke.
affirming my fears I was seated in the
exit row. *I'm not capable of saving us*
I thought. my seat neighbour and I
reviewed the card the stewardess handed us
and shrugged looking at the emergency
door. with no language in common I conveyed
with my eyes that as a man he would be
responsible for opening the door if need
arose. during takeoff it rattled in a way
that felt obviously ominous yet the stewardess
seated nearby was nonplussed and possibly
bored. these were probably routine sounds
or at least nothing to worry about. our pilot
wished us merry Christmas and regularly
informed us how high we had climbed. his

microphone was far too loud and startling.
meanwhile plane travel continues to astonish
and terrify me. you can plead aerodynamics
all you want but how do we stay in the sky?
I know I am more likely to be hit by a bus
or get cervical cancer or a melanoma. but
what if we are the next modern aviation mystery!
so many of us taking the risk of plane travel
the population of a small city is in the sky
at any given moment. my new community!
I love it, wish you were here. just in case
I prepare myself to die with these strangers
and look fondly around at my fellow passengers.
we may be written about in newspapers as
180 people who died in a plane over Vietnam
yet these were my people. we waited in lines
together, anticipated refreshments; i know
their holiday reads, those who unashamedly
wore practical zip-off pants, who smoked in the
airport smoking lounge, who disobeyed
announcements about turning their phone
to flight mode; we jumped at the pilot's
too-loud announcements. I will rest
in peace with a small smile on my face
thinking of their shitty singing.

zodiac buzz–killer

for Dorothea Lasky and Alex Dimitrov

spotify shared the star signs of my most listened to artists
they were mostly scorpios
what a genuine pleasure to know the astrology
of someone who is singing to you

celebrity compatibility astrology website
of course jesus was actually a pisces
(and actually a celebrity)
might be on the cusp of a major breakthrough
regarding his proclivity for fish
lots of celebrity sagittarius
would have thought more celebrities were leos

an analysis of compatibility between colleagues
through an app popular with queer adjacent friends
affirms everything already known to us
another story of a manager who ran the workplace
around everybody's star signs

feeling 'so seen' by instagram astrologers
categorised by meme-based content
feeling so millennial right now
(feeling so millennial inside this poem about astrology)
so safe to be inside this poem in one of twelve categories

the woolworths 1.25L soda water is a great deal
of course you would love that, a capricorn
something all signs agree on
is that the best bargain is a sodastream
a seamless segue from preferred beverage types of
millennials into
one for the literature lovers
two american poets take astrological aspects
and summarise into 240 characters or less
every writer loves a constraint
every body wants an interpretation
interpret me

a small pig smiled upon the year 2019
not a snake, I am a small dragon luckier than most
this new level of enlightenment is thanks
to a holiday to bali (would recommend)
this new level of commitment not only to the self but
also incense

rising sign helps to explain the sun sign
but mother doesn't remember the exact time of birth
sorry for getting all philosophical
no I like it it's rare to meet someone
who talks like this

the water not the wave

blacktown

not much to look at off the highway at oakhurst but
remember the old dairy used to be out there now
greg norman's bought it off the council property
developers and greg norman wants to build a golf
course and what greg wants greg gets today a quiet
circle of women down the creek words from the
reeds pelican across grey sky crow in the lone tree
speak of old ones as aunty sings music not from this
here time song connects wayback to children from
the old school paddock holds sorrow of parents who
watched at water's edge gather again and again on
this ground be present to heal the past

warrane

plaques etched with Dharug words on footpath at
circular quay trod by tourists come back stranger
do make bring speak well this coast could say
something too this shoreline has seen a whole lot
before whitefullas stuck a rag on a stick outside
mcdonald's and canoes sailed the manly fast ferry
route Barangaroo fished the harbour she broke
hubby's spear for working with arthur phillip drive
you wild that would they put anchors on plinths
as if to say look how much space we take up now
but saltwater tide ebbs on and on sure as ocean
reflects sky

merri

called south to write more and read more listen to
more music read more books talk to no one watch
everything be in the cold night escaping lips breath
turns into foglike something and wood fires burn
in little houses smoke rises across the rooftops alone
and far away from everything and everyone get up
so early and sweat everything out during a long run
ideally sit with the melancholy do not run from it
through romantic eyes see the beautiful nothing all
is made from the fullest nothing air of the creek
whirls down to the core

lake people i

here's how it goes or at least I think so and this is
the one story we're allowed to tell not with the
name of the bad man we weren't allowed to speak
of we were too scared to say it even now I'm not
allowed to say that's what nanny said to us and your
father knew it too so that wouldn't have been passed
down anyway but this one is well known and we
used to get told this version by granny but mum
told it a different way but it's been so long now
that I can't remember exactly what made their lake
stories different only that they would carry on about
it you never wanted to get them started on this story
in particular but any story really anyway I'll tell you
the one about the two brothers

lake people ii

hey yeah I'm here now can you tell me whereabouts
I'm meant to park and look for this thing I
definitely came in on the western side so from what
aunt told me I should just stay on the turnoff after
the pub and I'll come out on the western side of the
lake but now I'm here it's bigger than I remember
and I don't want to start walking around if I'm on
the wrong side yeah no there's no water I guess it
hasn't rained this season yet so I should be right to
walk around for a bit I just want to find that yep
you know exactly what I'm looking for I don't think
I've ever seen it full so it's kinda weird that people
water-ski here watched by those two brothers so
which way?

lake people iii

people abandon this place in winter lake is dry
white ochre bright expanding flat low down
through brush onto shore bullrushes at ankle height
waver bottles cans rubbish well beyond rustling
eucalypts join in ocean sound

lake people iv

got to be ours even though she's pale what do you
think can you sense the pelican spirit you'd have
to ask but sounds like she was talking about us
just now not proper that young one and she got
the story wrong it was me chased the spider away
not you and it wasn't my fault we couldn't save the
squirrel not that he deserved it anyway but it's the
law of Country now wait it was me with the spider
this time and you saved the squirrel from the eagle
other time no wonder these ones didn't pass on the
story proper way it happened to us and we can't
even get it right where do you think she's going
now that's the wrong way girl

which is good because love and connection to Country
are inseparable, care and understanding for a place that
seems outside of the body but is actually in and of it
interior self-love merging with exterior Country

the body can be a challenge
so I just believe what I once heard in a meditation

you are beautiful and everybody loves you

territories

authority figures

i

We all had to dodge the spears she'd been throwing.
The trail of the force that drove her womba led
us to the clearing where she hid. A source of
beautiful destruction that made her brilliant and
also made her mad. Some people didn't believe
she was possessed in this way, but it had taken
others before so everyone gathered to perform the
ceremony. Some of the camp dogs knew what was
about to happen and tried to get loose. They were
upset, but not possessed like she was. I raced up the
path determined to get away because I was scared
but also I was too young to see. Plus from there I
could see the way out. Lucky I escaped when I did
because police were approaching. Before I could
help myself the word 'police' croaked from my
mouth then I yelled again 'POLICE!'

ii

Rolling out colours to make an Aboriginal flag
from playdough. The yellow was ruined by blue
bits and the red had flecks of green. Childhood toys
given back to my older sibling and me, by a villain

who kept us captive at our childhood home. It had been a very long time since we had played together.

Our escape was by car—someone came to get us. Driving into the night we realised our lights weren't on, probably for the covert getaway. I switched on the headlights, just in time as we passed the police on the side of the road. They flashed their lights for us to stop. In our stationary beams, two children ran across the road. I noticed the fabric of the dressing gown one was wearing. Recognised it, I mean. It was mine from years ago. My sibling saw their mirror image.

The younger pair of us raced to the other side of the road, into the bushes out of sight.

Fleeing just like us.

every time I try to run, there I am again with myself

same as there is a way to keep opening eyes wider and
wider
to see more
to seek
there is also the inverse
look further within, different ways of closing eyes

or does it start other way round?

same as there is a way to keep looking deeper and deeper
within
there's more than just you
look beyond
find more ways to open up

either way the effect is the same
everything becomes more connected
more space reveals itself
the body is available to feel into it,

whatever that means

it feels warm and everything is touching
breaths meeting other breath

revolve

The earth rotates, holding my body down to it as it holds
the moon.

Margaret Atwood

Clear halo in deep navy, I first noticed it far from
home, or perhaps it finally found me. All this time I had
assumed I was being watched and here was proof: outline
of an eye, sky with no stars shining moon iris nightly.

Second time the orientation was more natural, immense.
I walked to sky's edge where town stops. Lay underneath
stars low and heavy enough to reach. The bright wanting
more.

All moon all the time, the third time. Celestial ceremony
captured in ochre. Made it not one but two, three, four
eyes that follow, even by day.

She walked Country before there was moon. Bearing a
torch she created day, but never made it back to her son.
What will we do if we lose that fire.

Finally we learned how it worked. Did we move or did
the moon. Or was it both. Anyway we drove towards it
that night. It was super, and the next one will be blue.

to yoke

let go of this heart
real estate reserved for memory ache
release long held certainties of land
unmoored I take Country with me wherever I go
I have to

sorrow morphs specific shapes
inhabits letters of your name
fills smallest of spaces
eye blinks closed

all was once Country and will return to ochre dust
reunion is possible once again   home

how to fall in love with your home town

think of the colours
shadows of the oval in the last day of term
dry yellow grass and bark breaking underfoot
against the blue edge of horizon on the outskirts of town
days where steely grey clouds hang low and eerie
no rain in them, just weight
from a distance it seems like everything was grey
yet up close purple, orange, gold
memory made of small gems and jewels

remember dewy morning first day of autumn air
winter dances frost across lawns
sunbeams coaxing out sweet scents
warming skin toward spring
endless summer days and nights lying down in cool grass
yet there are more than four seasons

think of the river
or if there was no river, the lake, or if there was no lake
or river, the mountains
and if there were neither of those just think of the sky
how it was always there to look up to
it knew everything then
knows everything still
including which way you will go next

territory

We are all leaving tracks. Walking is writing is weaving
is making, filling between lines of others. Time wrote angry
over land, diagonal tyres almost dendroglyphs. Tree clearing
left stray bark punctured by excavator teeth.

This Country is of pelican men, goolem goolem,
lake people and shadowy creatures.
Not exactly like bunyips, something from dry plains
still known by landscape, nadje creeping in on dusk
and Benabial who fled across the plains to Gariwerd,
shortly after white occupation and may still be there.

Yet none are strangers. And they speak the same.
Language lives inside land, flows river's veins,
pools into lake, remembered by hills and plains.

What else could the creek be babbling about?
Spoken by rustling grass, whispered through leaves
of red and blue gums, sobbed out by weeping
ironbark. Reading aloud the words of Country.

Instead of our language we were taught silence.
Generations kept quiet about the thing that happened
somewhere else, other than our bush, to peoples
who weren't related to us.

Country spells it out in dust: three points mean
emu, two equal dashes is kangaroo paws,
em dash for tail. Not all lines are straight, says the bend
of river down from the falls and curve of snake on sunny
rocks.

Turn to face mountain and tree, feel others
grown from earth. We resurrect. We are laiurg-mal
treading the same path, reading the same Country.
Spreading out across land, learning more words
to write the place with.

afterword

The body helps collect all the experiences that make up your life. It's the container for everything you hold to be true. But it's temporary. Country, as known in Aboriginal culture, lives beyond humans and holds a wisdom beyond our comprehension. And we learn from its immense memory.

I wrote an essay titled 'The Body Country' for the Faber Academy in 2019, and those formed the threads woven through this poetry collection. In the fragments I explore a tension between loving and knowing your body is important, while fearing its frailty and temporality. The body holds the essence of your self—whether you believe it to be eternal, living beyond here and now, or simply for the time you exist in human form—we all know the body doesn't last.

The fragments hold together poems reflecting further on this. How small we feel in nature, in front of the mountains, at lake's expansive edge or as we watch a carefree kangaroo bound through the dirt, drawing its tail through dust; or high up in a plane, observing life in miniature from above. How we persist in making connections in the symbols of the natural world, where we search for meaning, or have brief experiences that make us believe there might be more.

The idea of embodiment of Country speaks to the longing Aboriginal people feel to have our land back with unrestricted access to culture and Country. Many of our communities have been displaced and experience continual removal from traditional homelands to this day. Themes of reconnection and reclamation are explored in many of the ekphrastic poems about art, and more of the musings on home/Country and place. Anishinaabe artist Rebecca Belmore said she never feels homesick because she carries her culture with her. The sovereign self can never be homesick because she carries her connection to culture with her wherever she goes.

This book is an outcome of State Library Queensland's Black&Write! 2021 Fellowship program. I submitted the manuscript two years in a row before getting frustrated and giving up. My inner critic was telling me to give up completely, but I was encouraged by the editors to submit for the third time, so I pushed doubt aside and scrounged some determination to revisit the manuscript.

So while the essay threads are a more recent addition to the collection, the poems were written over a long period of time, almost ten years. Tracing my life through different cities, artworks, romances, heartbreaks, dreams, Country and moments of growth. They reflect a confidence in speaking up and speaking in my ancestral language.

Birds I heard at our farm during the first lockdowns in April 2020 inspired the suite of poems *Chorus,* which appeared in *The Suburban Review*'s Regional Voices edition. Including these more recent works unified and gave context to existing poems in the original manuscript. Something stronger and more resolved began to emerge, closer to what you are holding in your hands. I'm so grateful to people who believed in me and saw something in earlier versions. Try, fail, try again, fail again, try again. We aren't always winners, but effort is its own reward.

To me poetry and art-making is a process that is never completely finished, only resolved up to a point, ready to share with people for interpretation. While there is a haze of authorial intent, poetry has no fixed meaning, only what readers see and bring to understanding in a particular moment.

These marks on the page and what I hold in my body are a temporary expression, for the here and now. What is held in Country goes beyond.

I grasp through the immense universe for meaning that continues to elude me.

Wergaia Language words

Benabial—a native of giant stature
bulabul—ants
djubi-djubi—small bird
djinab—cockatoo
gauir—emu
gulum gulum / goolem goolem—dangerous stranger, wild
   blackfella
gurn-gurn—kookaburra
gurug—magpie
laiurg-mal—group of women
mindjun—grey kangaroo
nadje—a hairy little goblin
werbil—eagle

All language words are taken from Luise A. Hercus' *The
Languages of Victoria: A Late Survey in Two Parts*, which she

conducted with my great-grandmother Eleanor Jessie Pepper (Eleanor Jackson Stewart), alongside other Wergaia speakers, through the 1950s and 1960s. A more modern dictionary exists, and so may different translations or words. However, I intentionally wanted to reference the dictionary that my great-grandmother directly contributed to. I acknowledge and honour the ongoing language revitalisation work underway in community and on Country by Barengi Gadjin Land Council.

acknowledgements

Thank you to the editors and staff of the publications and competitions where some of the poems in this collection were previously published or performed: *Suburban Review*, *Rabbit Poetry Journal*, *Runway Journal*, Torrent Blossom at FirstDraft Sydney, *The Lifted Brow* Digital, The 2018 Overland Poetry Prize, Faber Writing Academy Sydney.

Thank you to Rose Hiscock and Virginia Lovett who welcomed me into their home in 2018 during a fellowship supported by Emerging Writers' Festival and State Library Victoria. You are a big part of this. Thanks also to the judges of the 2019 Writers Victoria Neilma Sidney Travel Fund.

The artists Nicole Foreshew and Amala Groom inspired the poems 'unceremonious' and 'dress code' respectively. Particular thanks to Nicole, Keith Munro, Clothilde Bullen and Nadeena Dixon whose mentorship while I worked in Sydney at Museum of Contemporary Art Australia both directly and indirectly supported me. The poem 'Blacktown' honours a site visit to the Blacktown Native Institution for MCA's C3West project.

Rebecca Belmore spoke about how she alleviates cultural homesickness at the 2022 Aabaakwad conference at the Venice Biennale. 'sidney nolan' is in response to Nolan's series of paintings about the Wimmera, as they are displayed in the Horsham Regional Art Gallery. 'counter narrative' is in response to NGV Australia at Federation Square. 'connecting' is inspired by the 2018 Sydney Biennale at Carriageworks. 'silent/song' was written during my first visit to Lutruwita for Dark Mofo in 2017 and refers to an artwork called 'Siren Song' which was blasted from the speakers of a helicopter at sunrise and sunset each day of the festival.

I first connected with the concept of the body as container as it appears in Haruki Murakami's novels, specifically in *Kafka on the Shore* but it is a motif that repeats through his work. 'You are beautiful and everybody loves you' (page 55) is a quote from a Louise Hay meditation tape from the 1980s. 'revolve' features a quote from Margaret Atwood's 1972 novel *Surfacing*. 'zodiac buzz-killer' refers to poets Dorothea Lasky and Alex Dimitrov's Twitter project Astro Poets.

Thank you to State Library of Queensland's black&write! team who read this manuscript in different iterations over the years and to the 2021 judges. To Grace Lucas-Pennington for the long, supportive phone calls. My editor Bianca Valentino for the reassurance and intuition about this collection—thank you so much. And gratitude to Jeanine Leane for guidance delivered at the right time.

I extend my respect to the communities whose countries I resided upon during writing and whose custodianship of Country enabled me safe creative passage on their land: to all Gadigal, Dharug, Wurundjeri, Boon Wurrung, Wotjobaluk, Wergaia, Djadwadjali, Palawa, Gunditjmara peoples. To the elders of these and other communities who I have met and worked with over the years: it is a privilege.

Thanks to OPIL. My colleagues at The University of Melbourne, particularly Elena del Mercato. Veronica Sullivan, Katie Hryce, Tegan Reeves, Nerida Ross, Talia Smith, Isabella Szukilojc, Jannah Quill, Nick Visser, Zena Cumpston: your funny, wise counsel on creativity and life inspired me as these poems came together across the years. My ride or die Alan Weedon. The Brains Trust: Gemma Robertson, Melissa DeLaney and Beck Pope.

And to my family.

Wergaia and Wemba Wemba writer Susie Anderson's poetry and non-fiction writing about art, artists, memory, place and love has been published widely in print and online. In 2018, she was a runner-up in the Overland Poetry Prize and awarded the Emerging Writers Fellowship at State Library Victoria; in 2019, she was awarded a Writers Victoria Neilma Sidney travel grant and undertook a residency with *Overland* literary journal. She edited the online journal *Tell Me Like You Mean It* Volume 4 for Australian Poetry and *Cordite Poetry Review* in 2020.

Susie was born in 1989 in Horsham, Victoria, and now lives on Boon Wurrung land. Find out more about her work at www.susan.fyi/

black&write!

black&write! is a national project run by State Library of Queensland with a dual focus on developing First Nations writers and editors, through editing internships and writing fellowships. Each year, black&write! offers two Fellowships for unpublished manuscripts by Aboriginal and/or Torres Strait Islander writers and these winning Fellows work closely with black&write! editors to develop their manuscripts for publication. For more information, go to the State Library of Queensland website:

www.slq.qld.gov.au/get-involved/
awards-and-fellowships/blackwrite/

hachette
AUSTRALIA

If you would like to find out more about Hachette Australia, our authors, upcoming events and new releases, you can visit our website or our social media channels:

hachette.com.au

 HachetteAustralia

 HachetteAus